Capital Cities of the United Kingdom

Cardiff

Anita Ganeri and Chris Oxlade

raintree
a Capstone company — publishers for children

Raintree is an imprint of Capstone Global Library Limited, a company incorporated in England and Wales having its registered office at 264 Banbury Road, Oxford, OX2 7DY – Registered company number: 6695582

www.raintree.co.uk
myorders@raintree.co.uk

Edited by Helen Cox Cannons
Designed by Philippa Jenkins
Original illustrations © Capstone Global Library Ltd 2016
Picture research by Eric Gohl
Production by Victoria Fitzgerald
Originated by Capstone Global Library Ltd
Printed and bound in China

ISBN 978 1 4747 2764 8
20 19 18 17 16
10 9 8 7 6 5 4 3 2 1

British Library Cataloguing in Publication Data
A full catalogue record for this book is available from the British Library.

Acknowledgements
We would like to thank the following for permission to reproduce photographs: Alamy: gbimages, 23, Graham Bell, 10, 13, Karl Robertson, 22, Sharon Lowe, 19, Stephen Saks Photography, 21; BigStockPhoto.com: BasPhoto, 14, Freedman, 15; Capstone: Oxford Designer and Illustrators, cover (map), 1, 5; © Collins Bartholomew Ltd 2016. Reproduced with permission of HarperCollins Publishers: 28; Courtesy of Tafwyl: 26; Dreamstime: Derek Phillips, 16; iStockphoto: David Callan, 11, liam4503, 9, susandaniels, 20; Library of Congress: 7; Newscom: Danita Delimont Photography/DanitaDelimont.com/Dave Bartruff, 12, Mirrorpix, 27; Shutterstock: Gail Johnson, 17, Leonid Andronov, 18, Neil Wigmore, 24, Philip Bird LRPS CPAGB, 8, 25, Tim Dobbs, cover, 4; Wikimedia: Seth Whales, 6.

Every effort has been made to contact copyright holders of material reproduced in this book. Any omissions will be rectified in subsequent printings if notice is given to the publisher.

Contents

Some words are shown in bold, **like this.**
You can find out what they mean by looking
in the glossary.

Where is Cardiff?

Every country has a capital city. The capital is the most important city. Cardiff is the capital city of Wales. The National Assembly for Wales is in Cardiff. It makes some of the laws for Wales.

Around 350,000 people live in Cardiff.

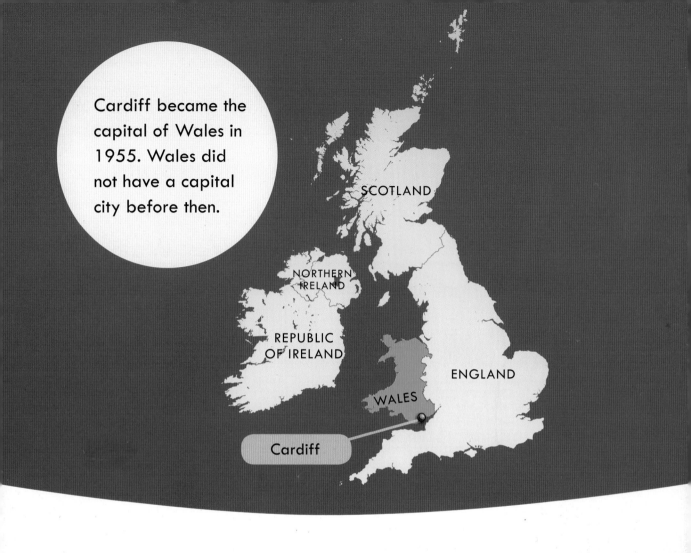

Cardiff became the capital of Wales in 1955. Wales did not have a capital city before then.

SCOTLAND

NORTHERN IRELAND

REPUBLIC OF IRELAND

ENGLAND

WALES

Cardiff

Cardiff is the biggest city in Wales. About one in ten people in Wales lives in Cardiff. That is twice as many as in the next biggest city, Swansea.

The story of Cardiff

Almost 2,000 years ago, the Romans built a **fort** at Cardiff. The **Normans** built the first castle at Cardiff about 900 years ago. This was the beginning of the city we see today.

Part of the Roman wall can still be seen today at Cardiff Castle.

One hundred years ago, Cardiff **docks** were full of ships carrying coal.

Around 200 years ago, coal and iron were found near Cardiff. Ships carried the coal and iron around the world. The city of Cardiff grew very quickly. It became the most important city in Wales.

Cardiff today

Today, Cardiff is a busy city. People come to Cardiff to work, shop, enjoy the restaurants and watch sport. There are many old buildings, such as Cardiff Castle. There are also many new buildings, such as the Millennium Stadium.

Queen Street is one of Cardiff's busy shopping streets.

8

City and County of
CARDIFF
Capital of Wales

Dinas a Sir
CAERDYDD
Prifddinas Cymru

Twinned with
Gefeilliwyd â

Hordaland
Lugansk
Nantes
Stuttgart
Xiamen

Caerdydd is the Welsh
name for Cardiff.

People from all over the world come to live and work in Cardiff. Lots of people visit Cardiff, too. All modern road signs and many shop signs are written in both English and Welsh.

The River Taff and Cardiff Bay

The River Taff runs through Cardiff city centre. The river flows from north to south, into the sea at Cardiff Bay. Boats can sail from the sea, up the river and right into the city centre.

Walkers and cyclists enjoy the path alongside the River Taff.

This yacht marina is inside Cardiff Bay.

Cardiff Bay is a huge lake. It is filled with **freshwater** from the River Taff and the River Ely. A wall, called the Cardiff Bay **Barrage**, runs across the Bay. It separates the Bay from the sea.

11

Cardiff Castle

Cardiff Castle is a popular place to visit. The main part of the castle is the Castle **Apartments.** The rooms look as if they could be in a fairy-tale palace. They have beautiful paintings and **ornaments.** There is a spectacular clock tower above the rooms.

The Great Hall in Cardiff Castle has a large fireplace.

A trebuchet was used to throw large stones or other objects at castle walls.

keep

trebuchet

Inside the castle walls, you can still see the castle's **Norman keep.** It stands on top of a mound of earth. You can also see a **medieval** weapon called a **trebuchet**.

Cardiff Bay and the Barrage

Cardiff Bay has lots of restaurants, cafés and walkways. You can also walk along the **Barrage**. A display in the Cardiff Bay Visitor Centre tells the story of the Bay and the Barrage.

Locks in the Barrage let ships pass between the Bay and the sea.

A walkway on the Barrage leads to the Barrage Sails.

The Barrage Sails are a sculpture that looks like the **bow** of a ship. There is an exhibition there about the famous explorer Captain Robert Scott. In 1910 Scott sailed from Cardiff in his ship *Terra Nova*. He was on his way to explore Antarctica.

15

Music and parks

The Senedd, at Cardiff Bay, is the home of the National Assembly for Wales. Close by is the Millennium Centre. Classical music concerts, opera and rock concerts are held there.

The Senedd building has a spectacular roof.

Many of the trees are so big that they are officially called "champion trees"!

Bute Park is a huge park next to Cardiff Castle and the city centre. It has nature trails to walk around and fitness trails to run around. The park also has sculptures to admire and lots of beautiful trees.

17

Cardiff's museums

The National Museum Cardiff has displays of dinosaur fossils and ancient rocks. It is also an art gallery, so there are priceless paintings there. You can see paintings by the famous artists Pablo Picasso and Vincent Van Gogh.

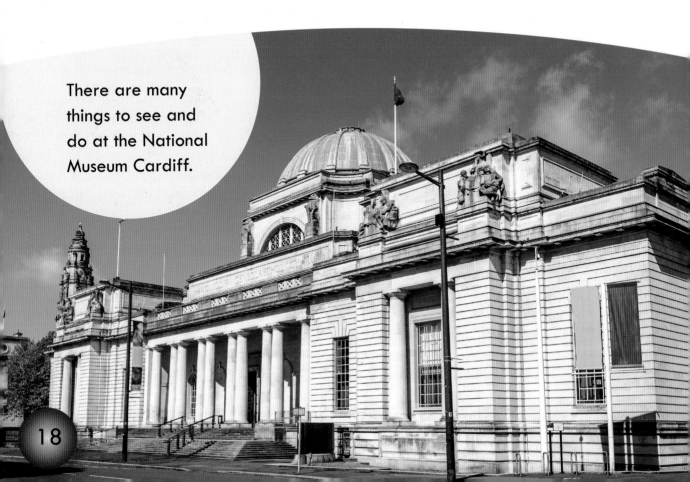

There are many things to see and do at the National Museum Cardiff.

18

You can watch craftspeople at work.

St Fagans National History Museum is an open-air museum. Experts have rebuilt old cottages, a farm and a school. They show how Welsh people lived and worked in the past.

19

Hidden gems

There are some amazing hidden sights in Cardiff. Look for the secret pictures painted on the **locks** at the Cardiff Bay **Barrage**. If you stand in exactly the right place, three yellow circles appear on the lock walls.

Artist Felice Varani painted the Barrage Circles.

Under Cardiff Castle, you can see clothes and equipment from World War II.

Underneath Cardiff Castle, there is a maze of ancient secret tunnels. These tunnels are dug deep into the walls. People sheltered, or hid, in these tunnels when Cardiff was bombed during **World War II**.

Shopping in Cardiff

The Indoor Market in Cardiff is packed with stalls. The stalls sell fruit and vegetables, meat and fish. You can also try some tasty local foods, such as Welsh cakes and **laverbread.** The shops of the Royal Arcade are near the market.

Cardiff's Indoor Market first opened in 1891.

The Craft in the Bay building is the place to go if you like crafts.

A craft gallery called Craft in the Bay is run by a group of craftspeople. There you can watch jewellers, potters and weavers at work. You can then have a go at making things yourself.

Sport in Cardiff

The Millennium Stadium stands on the banks of the River Taff. It is very close to the city centre. This stadium is the home of Welsh rugby. Here, up to 74,500 fans cheer on the Wales rugby team.

The Wales rugby team always plays in red.

Rafters enjoy paddling down the White Water course.

Close to Cardiff Bay there is an **artificial** river. It is called Cardiff International White Water. Water is pumped down a course to make bumpy waves, and canoeists and rafters go down it.

Festivals and celebrations

The Tafwyl Festival is a celebration of the Welsh language. Everyone at the festival speaks Welsh. The main event during the Festival is the Tafwyl Fair. It is a fun-filled weekend of music, sport and dancing.

Around one in ten people living in Cardiff speak Welsh.

People wave the flag of St David and wear traditional costumes at the Saint David's Day parade.

Saint David is the **patron saint** of Wales. On 1 March every year, people celebrate Saint David's Day. There is a parade through the city centre. The parade winds its way towards Cardiff Castle.

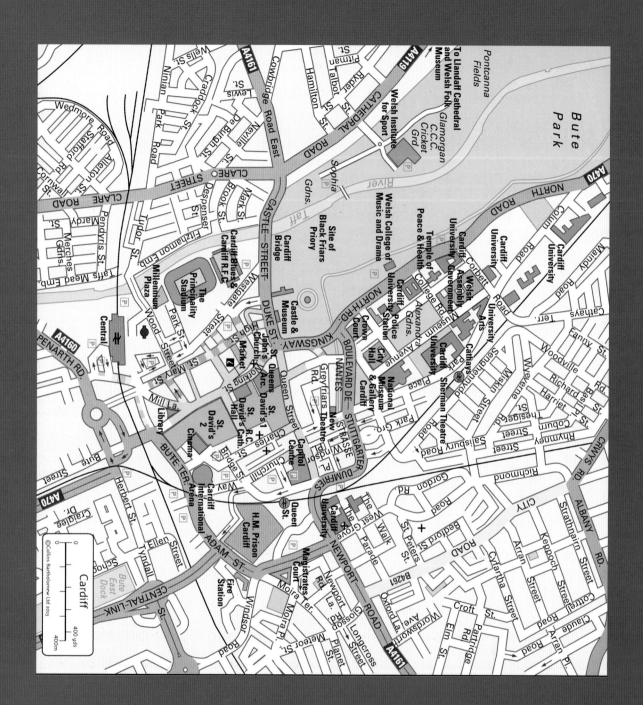

Glossary

apartment set of private rooms in a large building

artificial man-made to seem real

barrage wall that holds back seawater as the tide rises and falls

dock place where ships are built or where they are loaded and unloaded

fort building with strong walls that protects people inside from attack

freshwater water that does not contain salt

keep strong tower inside a castle

laverbread type of bread made from boiled seaweed and oats

lock small part of a canal, with gates at each end, which lifts boats and ships from a lower level to a higher level

medieval having to do with the period of history between AD 500 and 1450, called the Middle Ages

Normans people who came over to England and Wales from Normandy in France in 1066

patron saint saint who is thought to protect the people of a country

trebuchet medieval weapon that hurled rocks through the air

World War II war fought by many of the world's countries between 1939 and 1945

29

Find out more

Books

City Guide to Cardiff, Trevor Price (Amazon Publishing, 2014)

Hometown History Cardiff, Sue Barrow (Home Town World, 2010)

Let's Visit Wales, Annabelle Lynch (Franklin Watts, 2015)

Websites

www.cardiffbay.co.uk
This site tells you all about the things you can see, and events to go to, at the waterfront in Cardiff Bay.

www.tafwyl.org/en
This website tells you all about the Tafwyl Festival, held in July each year, which celebrates the Welsh language.

www.visitcardiff.com
This is the official website for visitors to Cardiff, with lots of information on sights to see, places to eat and events.

Places to visit

Places mentioned in the book
Cardiff Castle, Castle Street, Cardiff CF10 3RB
www.cardiffcastle.com

National Museum and Gallery of Wales, Cathays
Park, Cardiff CF10 3NP
www.museumwales.ac.uk/cardiff

St Fagans National History Museum, Cardiff CF5 6XB
www.museumwales.ac.uk/stfagans

More places to visit
Doctor Who Experience, Discovery Quay, Porth Teigr,
Cardiff Bay, Cardiff CF10 4GA
www.doctorwho.tv/events/doctor-who-experience

Techniquest Science and Discovery Centre, Stuart
Street, Cardiff CF10 5BW
www.techniquest.org

The Cardiff Story, The Old Library, The Hayes, Cardiff
CF10 1BH
cardiffstory.com

Index